THE MONK ON A MARKETING STREET

Let's Unleash the Game of Madness in Marketing

Dedicated to all the marketers out there in the market who are continuously working to send the right product to the right audience and changing the lives of billions of people and business owners with their skillsets.

Acknowledgement

- Arti Mam
- Jaswinder Singh

Index

The secret of doing business is knowing something that nobody else knows.

-Aristotle

As a person with an entrepreneur mindset, I've always believed that the secret to success in business is knowing something that nobody else knows. In a competitive marketplace, it's essential to differentiate ourselves from the competition and offer something unique that sets us apart. This can be in the form of a proprietary product or service, a specialized skill set or technology, or simply a unique perspective on the market and its needs.

Having this kind of knowledge or expertise can give us a competitive edge, allowing us to attract and retain customers and command higher prices for our offerings. However, it's not enough to have unique knowledge alone; we must also effectively communicate the value of what we have to offer to our target audience.

This is where marketing comes in. As a person with growth-oriented entrepreneur mindset, I'm always exploring new ways to build awareness and interest in my business and its unique value proposition (USP). This includes creating compelling content that showcases my knowledge and expertise, leveraging social media and other digital marketing channels to reach my target audience, and partnering with other businesses or influencers in my industry to amplify my message.

Ultimately, the key to success in business is a combination of having unique knowledge or expertise and effectively marketing that knowledge to our target audience. By doing so, we can differentiate our business from the competition, attract and retain customers, and achieve our growth and profitability goals. As an entrepreneur, I'm constantly striving to learn and improve, and I'm excited to see where this combination of unique knowledge and effective marketing will take me and my business in the future.

In order to become rich, your fear of poverty must be more motivating than your greed for money.

-Prashant Mehetre

As a non-fiction author who writes on business, marketing, and the entrepreneur mindset, I believe that the quote speaks to the importance of mindset in achieving financial success. Fear and greed are two of the most powerful motivators for humans. behavior, and in the context of entrepreneurship, both can be harnessed to achieve success. However, in my experience, the fear of poverty is often a stronger motivator than the desire for wealth. This is because the fear of poverty is rooted in a deep-seated need for security and stability. Entrepreneurs who have experienced financial hardship or instability in their lives, they are often more driven to succeed. because they are acutely aware of the consequences of failure. On the other hand, the desire for wealth can be a fleeting motivation that fades over time. Greed can lead to short-sighted decisions and a lack of Focus on the long-term goals that are necessary for sustained success.

Therefore, as a marketer, with an entrepreneur mindset, it is essential to cultivate a healthy fear of failure and a strong work ethic to overcome any challenges that may arise. This mindset can help ensure that you are motivated by the right factors, and that you make decisions that are in line with your long-term goals.

The first rule of marketing is: "If they want to die, sell them the death."

Prashant Mehetre

As an author, entrepreneur, and hardcore marketer, I believe that this quote speaks to the importance of understanding your audience's needs and desires.

As a growth hacker, my ultimate goal is to sell my products or services to my target audience. However, I understand that in order to do this effectively, I must first understand their needs and desires. If I try to sell them something that doesn't align with their needs and desires, I am likely to fail.

The first rule of marketing is to never try to sell your audience something that they don't want or need. This is because if you try to sell them something that is irrelevant or doesn't resonate with them, they will quickly lose interest and move on.

On the other hand, if you can tap into your audience's needs and desires and sell them something that truly solves a problem or fulfils a desire, you are more likely to succeed. In this sense, the quote "if they want to die, sell them the death." means that if you try to sell something that is irrelevant or doesn't align with your audience's needs, you are essentially selling them a "death" sentence for your business.

Therefore, as a marketer, it is important to listen to your audience, understand their needs and desires, and create products or services that align with them. By doing so, you can build trust, establish a loyal customer base, and ultimately achieve long-term success.

The market never runs on emotions; it runs on stats and figures, but market runs for the emotions.

Prashant Mehetre

As an author, entrepreneur, growth hackers and hardcore marketer, I believe that this quote encapsulates the essence of marketing in a single sentence.

Marketing is a field that is often associated with emotions, but at its core, it is driven by numbers and statistics. As marketers, we are constantly analyzing data to better understand our target audience and improve our marketing efforts. We use metrics such as click-through rates, conversion rates, and customer lifetime value to make informed decisions and drive results.

However, despite the importance of data and statistics in marketing, it is ultimately emotions that drive consumer behavior. People buy products and services not just because of their features and benefits but also because of how they make them feel. Marketing campaigns that tap into emotions such as happiness, fear, or nostalgia are often the most successful because they resonate with consumers on a deeper level.

Therefore, while data and statistics are critical to the success of marketing, it is emotions that ultimately drive sales. As marketers, it is our job to use data to inform our strategies and tactics while also creating emotional connections with our audience. By striking this balance, we can create marketing campaigns that are both effective and memorable and ultimately drive long-term success for our businesses.

You stop loving girls when you start loving markets.

Prashant Mehetre

As, an author, growth hacker entrepreneur, and marketer, I believe that this quote speaks to the all-encompassing nature of business and entrepreneurship.

When you are deeply involved in business and entrepreneurship, your focus shifts to building and growing your venture. You are constantly thinking about your target audience, market trends, and ways to improve your product or service. In this sense, it can be difficult to devote as much time and attention to personal relationships.

However, I do not believe that this means that you have to completely give up on personal relationships or stop loving girls. Rather, it's about finding a balance between your business pursuits and your personal life.

In fact, I believe that having a healthy personal life can actually enhance your business success. Having strong relationships can provide emotional support, inspiration, and motivation, all of which can help you stay focused and driven in your entrepreneurial endeavors.

Ultimately, it is up to each individual to find the right balance between their business pursuits and personal lives. While entrepreneurship and business can be all-consuming, it is important to also priorities personal relationships and self-care in order to achieve long-term success and happiness.

Nothing can explain reality better than reality itself.

-Prashant Mehetre

As an author, marketer, growth hacker and entrepreneur, I believe that this quote speaks to the power of direct experience and firsthand knowledge.

No matter how much we read, study, or learn from others, there is no substitute for experiencing something firsthand. When we experience something ourselves, we gain a deeper understanding of it that cannot be conveyed through words or secondhand accounts.

In business and entrepreneurship, this principle is particularly relevant. We can read books, attend seminars, and listen to experts, but ultimately, it is our own experience that will teach us the most valuable lessons. This is why trial and error is such an important part of the entrepreneurial journey; it is through our failures and successes that we learn and grow the most.

At the same time, it is important to approach our experiences with an open mind and a willingness to learn. Even when things don't go as planned, we can still learn valuable lessons that will help us in the future.

In summary, the quote "nothing can explain reality better than reality itself" reminds us that while learning from others is valuable, direct experience is the most powerful teacher. By embracing our experiences and learning from them, we can gain a deeper understanding of ourselves, our businesses, and the world around us.

Instead of being the master of machines, be the master of markets.

Prashant Mehetre

As an author, entrepreneur, and marketer, I believe that this quote highlights the importance of focusing on the market and customers rather than just the technology or tools used in business.

In today's digital age, it is easy to get caught up in the latest technology and tools. While these can be valuable resources for businesses, they are ultimately just meaning to an end. The real goal of any business should be to serve its customers and meet their needs.

Being the master of the market means understanding your target audience, their needs, and how to reach and engage with them effectively. This requires a deep understanding of the market, including trends, competition, and consumer behavior.

When businesses focus solely on the technology or tools they use, they risk losing sight of the bigger picture. They may end up creating products or services that do not meet the needs of their customers or fail to effectively communicate their value proposition.

On the other hand, businesses that are focused on mastering the market are more likely to succeed in the long term. By putting the needs of their customers first, they can create products and services that truly resonate with their audience and build a loyal customer base.

In summary, the quote "Instead of being the master of the machine, be the master of the market" reminds us that technology and tools are just means to an end. The real goal of any business should be to serve its customers and meet their needs, and this requires a deep understanding of the market and how to effectively engage with it.

Manufacturers and engineers have produced many of the finest products ever. Many great products will come and go in the upcoming future, too. But there won't be any other product as fine, stubborn, difficult, and complex to understand as the one named "Market," and the marketers own it, not the manufacturers, engineers, and product owners.

-Prashant Mehetre

As, an author, entrepreneur, and marketer, I believe that this quote speaks to the unique complexity and intricacy of the market, as well as the important role that marketers play in shaping and understanding it.

Unlike other products that are designed and manufactured by engineers and product owners, the market is an ever-evolving entity that is shaped by a wide range of factors, including consumer behavior, economic conditions, and cultural trends.

Marketers are the ones who truly understand the market, as they are responsible for identifying consumer needs and preferences, analyzing market data, and developing strategies to promote products and services.

However, despite their expertise, marketers must navigate a complex and ever-changing landscape, where success is not always guaranteed. The market can be fickle and unpredictable, and even the most experienced marketers must constantly adapt and refine their strategies to stay ahead of the competition.

At the same time, the market is a truly remarkable and innovative creation, with the power to transform entire industries and change the course of history. By understanding and harnessing the power of the market, marketers have the ability to shape the future and drive positive change in the world.

In summary, the quote **"there is no other product as finest, stubborn, difficult, and complicated to understand as the product named 'market', and the marketers own it, not the manufacturers, engineers, and product owners"**

highlights the unique complexity and importance of the market, as well as the critical role that marketers play in shaping and understanding it. By understanding the market and harnessing its power, marketers can drive innovation, promote positive change, and achieve success in today's fast-paced and ever-changing business environment.

However, I can provide a deeper explanation of the quote: "There is no other product as finest, stubborn, difficult, and complicated to understand as the product named 'market', and the marketers own it, not the manufacturers, engineers, and product owners."

The market is a complex and ever-changing entity, shaped by a wide range of factors that are often difficult to predict and understand. Unlike other products that are designed and manufactured by engineers and product owners, the market is shaped by consumer behavior, economic conditions, cultural trends, and a host of other factors.

As a result, the market is not a static entity that can be easily understood or controlled. Rather, it is a dynamic and ever-evolving landscape that requires a deep understanding of human psychology, data analysis, and market trends to navigate successfully.

Marketers are uniquely positioned to understand and navigate the market, as they are responsible for identifying consumer needs and preferences, analyzing market data, and developing strategies to promote products and services. They must be able to adapt quickly to changing market conditions and consumer behavior, and they must have the skills and knowledge to identify emerging trends and opportunities.

At the same time, marketers must also be able to communicate effectively with other stakeholders, such as product owners, engineers, and manufacturers. They must be able to explain market trends and consumer behavior in a way that these stakeholders can understand, and they must be able to collaborate effectively with these stakeholders to develop products and services that meet the needs of consumers.

In short, the market is a complex and dynamic entity that requires a deep understanding of consumer behavior, data analysis, and market trends to navigate successfully. Marketers are uniquely positioned to understand and navigate the market, and they must have the skills and knowledge to communicate effectively with other stakeholders and collaborate effectively to develop products and services that meet the needs of consumers.

In conclusion, the quote "there is no other product as finest, stubborn, difficult, and complicated to understand as the product named 'market', and the marketers own it, not the manufacturers, engineers, and product owners" speaks to the unique complexity and importance of the market, as well as the critical role that marketers play in shaping and understanding it. By understanding and harnessing the power of the market, marketers can drive innovation, promote positive change, and achieve success in today's fast-paced and ever-changing business environment.

Everything that you are watching on the glass screen is either planned, scripted, manipulated, biased, or dominated.

-Prashant Mehetre.

As, an author and entrepreneur, I believe that this quote highlights the importance of being critical and discerning consumers of media.

In today's digital age, we are constantly bombarded with information and media through our screens, whether it's through television, social media, or the internet. While this can be a valuable source of information and entertainment, it is important to remember that not all of it is unbiased or objective.

As the quote suggests, much of what we see on the screen is planned, scripted, manipulated, biased, or dominated. This can be due to a variety of factors, including media ownership, advertising pressures, cutthroat competition of bringing audience/generating advertising revenue and editorial biases.

As consumers of media, it is important to approach everything we see with a critical eye. We should ask ourselves who is producing the content, what their motivations and biases may be, and whether the information presented is factually accurate.

At the same time, we should also seek out diverse sources of information and perspectives. By exposing ourselves to a variety of viewpoints and sources, we can gain a more well-rounded understanding of the world and make more informed decisions.

In summary, the quote "everything that you are watching on the glass screen is either planned, scripted, manipulated, biased, or dominated" reminds us to be critical and discerning consumers of media. By approaching everything we see with a critical eye and seeking out diverse sources of information, we can better understand the world around us and make more informed decisions.

Going out of the box doesn't work every time; in fact, it has become so overrated. Staying focused inside the circle is a new business and life hack.

-Prashant Mehetre

As, an author, growth hacker, entrepreneur, and marketer, I believe that this quote highlights the importance of staying focused and grounded in our goals and objectives, rather than constantly seeking to "think outside the box".

In recent years, there has been a lot of emphasis on innovation and creativity in business and life. While these can be valuable traits, they are not the only factors that lead to success.

Sometimes, the most effective strategy is simply to stay focused and committed to the tasks and goals at hand, rather than constantly seeking to reinvent the wheel. This is particularly true in today's fast-paced and ever-changing business environment, where it can be easy to get distracted by new ideas and trends.

Staying focused inside the circle means identifying what works and what doesn't work for your business or life, and focusing your efforts on improving and optimizing those areas. This may involve embracing proven strategies and processes, rather than constantly seeking to innovate.

Of course, this does not mean that businesses and individuals should never seek to think outside the box or try new things. Rather, it suggests that these efforts should be balanced with a healthy dose of realism and practicality.

In summary, the quote **"going out of the box doesn't work every time; in fact, it has become so overrated that staying focused inside the circle is a new business and life hack"** reminds us of the importance of staying focused and grounded in our goals and objectives rather than constantly seeking to reinvent the wheel. By identifying what works and what doesn't and focusing our efforts on improving and optimizing those areas, we can achieve success in both business and life.

The best product is one that changes customers lives and the company's balance sheet.

-Prashant Mehetre

As, an author, growth hacker, entrepreneur, and marketer, I believe that this quote emphasizes the importance of creating products that not only satisfy customers' needs but also generate profits for the company.

In today's competitive business environment, creating a product that truly resonates with customers is not enough. To be successful in the long term, a product must also be financially viable and contribute to the company's bottom line.

At the same time, a product that solely focuses on generating profits and ignores customers' needs is unlikely to succeed. To truly stand out in today's market, a product must have a meaningful impact on customers' lives and solve a real problem for them.

The best products are those that strike a balance between these two objectives—they are both transformative for customers and profitable for the company. By creating products that truly change customers' lives, companies can build strong customer loyalty and generate sustainable and recurring profits over the long term.

In summary, the quote *"the best product is that which changes customers' lives and companies' balance sheets"* highlights the importance of creating products that not only satisfy customers' needs but also generate profits for the company. By striking a balance between these two objectives, companies can create products that truly stand out in today's competitive market and build a loyal customer base over time.

It's the bedrock theory of marketing and, paraphrasing somewhat, essentially points out that the first rule of marketing is that you are not the market. All your thoughts, feelings and immediate responses to things like advertising, price and packaging are not just incorrect – they are dangerous.

If you are born in a capitalist country and you have said no to doing a business, it means you have said no to becoming rich.

-Prashant Mehetre

In my opinion, if I am born in a capitalist country and decide not to pursue business ventures, I believe that it means I am saying no to becoming rich. From my perspective, starting a business is seen as the primary route to acquiring wealth within a capitalist system.

I think that by declining business opportunities, I am essentially giving up on the potential financial gains that come with entrepreneurship. In my view, the most reliable and direct path to accumulating wealth in a capitalist society is through creating and managing a successful business.

I understand that individuals have different perspectives and definitions of what it means to be rich or successful. However, I believe that entrepreneurship offers the most promising opportunities for financial prosperity. While I acknowledge that other avenues such as investing, high-paying professions, or personal fulfillment may also lead to wealth and success, I personally see starting a business as the most direct path to achieving my desired level of wealth.

Human minds are evil. And there are fucking 7 billion evil minds alive in the world right now. Billions of evil minds have passed away from this land, leaving their impact behind, which we are witnessing and experiencing in the form of today's society and market. No wonder the society and market is so tough to understand and survive in.

-Prashant Mehetre

The statement "human minds are evil" is a controversial one that is open to interpretation and debate. However, the idea that there are billions of minds in the world, many of which may be driven by negative or harmful impulses, is certainly a compelling one.

When it comes to the market, it is true that the actions and behaviors of consumers can be difficult to predict and understand. This is because each individual brings their own unique set of biases, beliefs, and experiences to the table, which can shape their purchasing decisions and overall behavior in the marketplace.

Furthermore, the competitive nature of the market can often bring out the worst in people, as businesses and individuals alike vie for attention, resources, and market share. This can lead to cutthroat tactics, dishonesty, and even outright manipulation, all of which can make it difficult for honest and ethical businesses to survive and thrive.

However, it is important to note that not all individuals and businesses in the market are inherently evil or malicious. There are many examples of businesses and individuals who priorities integrity, honesty, and social responsibility in their dealings, and who work to create value for their customers and society as a whole.

Ultimately, while the market may be a complex and challenging environment to navigate, it is important to recognize that it is driven by the actions and behaviors of individual consumers and businesses. By understanding and respecting the needs and values of these stakeholders and prioritizing ethics and integrity in all business dealings, it is possible to succeed and thrive in the market while still upholding a positive and socially responsible image.

Marketing is all about an art of connecting the dots by looking forward.

Prashant Mehetre

As a business author focused on marketing, I firmly believe that marketing is all about connecting the dots by looking forward. In today's ever-evolving business landscape, it is crucial for marketers to anticipate trends, understand customer behavior, and proactively adapt their strategies to stay ahead of the curve. By looking forward and connecting those dots, marketers can unlock opportunities for growth and success.

Steve Jobs once famously said, "You can't connect the dots by looking forward. You can only connect them by looking backward." While this statement primarily applies to personal experiences and life choices, it holds profound significance when applied to the realm of marketing and business.

To fully comprehend the connection between these two ideas, we must first grasp the essence of Steve Jobs' quote. Jobs emphasized the importance of retrospection, learning from past experiences, and understanding the interconnectedness of events. By reflecting on the past, we can gain valuable insights that guide us in successfully navigating the future.

In the realm of marketing, this concept aligns perfectly with the notion of connecting the dots by looking forward. While it may seem contradictory at first, the true power of connecting the dots lies in combining the wisdom gained from hindsight with the ability to anticipate future trends and consumer demands.

When marketers look forward, they have the opportunity to identify emerging technologies, changing consumer preferences, and market shifts. By staying informed and adaptive, marketers can strategically connect these dots, leveraging past experiences as a foundation for future success.

Looking back at past marketing campaigns and strategies allows marketers to analyze what worked and what didn't. It enables them to identify patterns, consumer behavior trends, and market dynamics that have shaped their industry. This retrospective analysis provides valuable insights that can be used to shape future marketing initiatives.

However, merely relying on historical data and insights is not enough. In today's rapidly evolving market, success requires the ability to connect the dots by looking forward. This involves envisioning potential future scenarios, embracing innovation, and predicting consumer needs before they arise.

By combining retrospective wisdom with forward-thinking strategies, marketers can anticipate market shifts and develop proactive campaigns that resonate with their target audience. This approach empowers businesses to stay one step ahead of the competition and position themselves as industry leaders.

In this context, connecting the dots by looking forward becomes an art form. It requires a deep understanding of market dynamics, a keen eye for emerging trends, and the ability to spot patterns before they become mainstream. Marketers must gather market intelligence, conduct market research, and leverage data analytics to inform their decisions and connect the dots effectively.

Furthermore, this approach to connecting the dots by looking forward encourages marketers to embrace agility and adaptability. It demands a willingness to experiment, take calculated risks, and iterate on strategies as the market evolves. By continuously evaluating and adjusting their efforts, marketers can ensure their campaigns remain relevant and impactful in an ever-changing business landscape.

In conclusion, as a business author focused on marketing, I firmly believe that marketing is all about connecting the dots by looking forward. By combining the wisdom gained from past experiences with the ability to anticipate future trends and consumer behavior, marketers can unlock growth and success. Steve Jobs' famous quote reminds us of the importance of retrospection, while emphasizing that true connections are made when we apply those insights to our future endeavors. So, let us embrace the power of looking back to move forward and connect the dots that lead to remarkable marketing achievements.

Your Pain, Your Passion, Your Aggression, your regrets and all must be seen in only one thing – And that is profit column of your balance sheet.

- *Prashant Mehetre*

In my perspective, I believe that all of my pain, passion, aggression, and regrets should be channeled towards one singular objective: maximizing the profit column on my balance sheet. From my point of view, the ultimate measure of success lies in the financial gains I can achieve.

I strongly believe that every aspect of my life, whether it be the challenges I face, the things I am passionate about, the determination I exhibit, or the mistakes I may have made, should be directed towards generating profit. I see the balance sheet as the ultimate indicator of accomplishment and progress in a capitalist society.

By prioritizing the profit column, I believe that I can harness the full potential of my emotions, experiences, and efforts to drive financial success. It is my conviction that by focusing solely on the pursuit of profit, I can ensure that my endeavors yield tangible and measurable results.

It's important to note that this viewpoint places significant emphasis on financial gains and may overlook other aspects of life such as personal fulfillment, relationships, and overall well-being. However, from my perspective, the profit column serves as the ultimate reflection of my achievements and represents the culmination of my pain, passion, aggression, and regrets in a capitalist society.

Just keep your heart clean & let anything other than it be dirty. Whatever it may be career, life, business and all. All other things can be regaining to its original shape and shape but heart can't.

-Prashant Mehetre

Whoever is reading this quote and whoever you are—a marketer, an entrepreneur, or a business owner—this quote is for you. In fact, I have written for every ordinary, extraordinary fellow who wants to live life to the fullest.

Many times, a situation of hardships, difficulties, and crises comes into the life of an entrepreneur, product owner, or businessman, and he literally thinks of giving up. He thinks he has messed up everything and starts losing faith in his confidence. He thinks he has messed up everything in life behind the goals, ambitions, and dreams and ends up getting into depression many times.

During those hard days, everything looks spoiled, and we couldn't find a ray of hope to proceed from this situation. We felt stuck. We start blaming our fortune and cursing our own decisions, ending up with nothing but depression.

All I wanted to say to whoever has been witnessing this right now or might have witnessed, all these things pass with time. These hardships are like dark clouds that definitely fade away after some time.

But one thing that I wanted to convey through my quote was to Keep only one thing neat and clean, which will drag you back through every kind of hardship in life, no matter how cruel it is, and that is your heart.

Your clean, unbiased, holy, and pious heart, which thinks positively and great about everyone and everything, will drag you back on the right track, even from hell. So, that why keep your heart clean and let other things be dirty. Don't worry

Thank You...